ISBN 978-0-282-64172-6
PIBN 10860259

1 MONTH OF
FREE
READING

at

www.ForgottenBooks.com

By purchasing this book you are eligible for one month membership to ForgottenBooks.com, giving you unlimited access to our entire collection of over 1,000,000 titles via our web site and mobile apps.

To claim your free month visit:
www.forgottenbooks.com/free860259

English
Français
Deutsche
Italiano
Español
Português

www.forgottenbooks.com

Mythology Photography **Fiction**
Fishing Christianity **Art** Cooking
Essays Buddhism Freemasonry
Medicine **Biology** Music **Ancient
Egypt** Evolution Carpentry Physics
Dance Geology **Mathematics** Fitness
Shakespeare **Folklore** Yoga Marketing
Confidence Immortality Biographies
Poetry **Psychology** Witchcraft
Electronics Chemistry History **Law**
Accounting **Philosophy** Anthropology
Alchemy Drama Quantum Mechanics
Atheism Sexual Health **Ancient History**
Entrepreneurship Languages Sport
Paleontology Needlework Islam
Metaphysics Investment Archaeology
Parenting Statistics Criminology
Motivational

A Study of Fugue Writing

Based on Bach's Well-tempered Clavichord

QUINCY PORTER

Published by
Loomis & Co.
Boston, Mass.

A Study of Fugue Writing

Based on Bach's Well-tempered Clavichord

QUINCY PORTER

Published by
Loomis & Co.
201 Devonshire St.
Boston, Mass.

281088

Introductory

The object of this little book is to provide a method by which a student may discover for himself, as he examines the fugues of the Well-tempered Clavichord, principles and restrictions of Bach's fugal style sufficient to enable him to write fugues in two, three or four voices which might (to speak optimistically) have pleased the great master if they had been written by one of his pupils. It is the intention of the text to make Bach himself the teacher, to as great an extent as is possible at this late date.

It has long been the contention of the author that musical composition can not be taught successfully simply by furnishing the student with a set of rules. A student enjoys having definite rules to follow and often completes a course with a good mark though he may not in the process discover one useful principle. No one would be interested in music if it could be formulated into rules. The great composers, as we shall find in the case of Bach, were interested in past styles only when they were useful to them. They broke rules or made new ones to fit their own convictions. It is useful for a student to study restrictions of a given style, provided he remembers at all times that he is studying only one of many styles in an art which is ever-changing. Bach, endowed with a musical intelligence and intuition scarcely ever equalled, had a grasp of the basic principles of musical composition which has not yet ceased to cause wonder. We have not yet succeeded in formulating all of his practices. There is still much to discover, and it is important for the individual to discover that which is of greatest value to him. Hence the method of this text.

A study of this kind presupposes a solid knowledge of classic harmony, coupled with facility in modulations to near keys. A student trained to make harmonizations of chorals in the style of Bach should be sufficiently equipped from this standpoint. The author believes that a study of modal counterpoint preceding the present study would be of inestimable value, as the principles of contrapuntal writing stand out in clearer relief when harmonic principles are further in the background, as in the works of di Lasso or Palestrina.

Each student should provide himself with both volumes of the Well-tempered Clavichord, and with a loose-leaf notebook containing plain sheets as well as staff paper.

Abbreviations

A.	Answer	Exp.	Exposition	S.D.	Subdominant
C.Exp.	Counterexposition	Inv.	Inversion	T.	Tonic
C.S.	Countersubject	Mod.	Modulating	WTC	Well-tempered Clavi-
D.	Dominant	Ped.	Pedal Point		chord
Ep.	Episode	Rel.	Relative		

Roman numerals show the volume number; the figure following, the fugue number; and the *italic* figures, the measure numbers in references to examples in Bach. For example: I 5 *5-8* means WTC Vol. I, Fugue 5, measures 5 to 8.

PART I
OUTLINE FOR STUDY
(Section references are to Part II)

I. **Subject** § 1
   A. Kinds § 2
      1. Non-mod. S.
      2. Mod. S.
   B. Analysis of S.'s §§ 3-12
      1. *a.* Number of voices § 4
         b. Range of S. § 4
      2. Note of T. scale at start § 5
      3. Simplest harmony suggested § 6
      4. Last note § 7
         a. Which note of T. or D. scale?
         b. Non-mod. or Mod. S.?
      5. Study of rhythm § 8
         a. Phrasing; rhythmic cells
         b. Continuity factors
         c. Rhythmic characteristics
      6. Study of melody § 9
         a. Climactic note(s); reasons for choice
         b. Striking characteristics
      7. General observations
II. **Answer**
   A. To Non-mod. S. § 13
      1. Real
      2. Tonal
   B. To Mod. S. § 14
      1. Start real or tonal
      2. Drop of one tone
   C. Points at which A. may start § 15
      1. Non-stretto fugue
      2. Stretto fugue
III. **Continuation of first voice**
   A. Continuity § 16
   B. Countersubject § 17
   C. Usefulness of C.S. § 18
IV. **Structure of fugue** § 19
   A. Main Exp. § 20
      1. Order of entrances § 21
      2. Spacing of entrances § 22
   B. Short Ep. to C. Exp. (?)
   C. C. Exp. § 23
   D. Ep. to Rel. § 24
   E. Exp. in Rel. x 25
   F. Ep. leading to G or H § 24
   G. Exp. in S.D. § 25
   H. Exp. in Rel. of S.D. § 25

x

PART II
SECTIONS FOR REFERENCE

1. It goes almost without saying that a good fugue cannot be built on a bad S. A detailed study of all the S.'s of Vol. I can be made with profit, continuing if possible through the S.'s of Vol. II. Though Bach's S.'s are amazingly varied in character and mood, there are principles to which he adheres with great consistency. These will become more apparent after the study of a number of S.'s. Every standpoint from which the S.'s are studied should give ideas helpful to the student in the construction of original S.'s. Before attempting to write his own, the student should refer to §§ 31-35.

2. A Non-mod. S. almost invariably makes a feeling of cadence to the T. of the original key at its conclusion. A Mod. S. concludes on the T. of the D. key, with a definite feeling of modulation to that key. These are the only two types of S. to be found in the WTC.

3. Illustrations of the analysis of S.'s I 1, 2 and 3 are given in §§ 10-12, made in accordance with the outline: I B.

4. A comparison of the range (in semitones) with the number of voices in the various fugues will call attention to the fact that the more voices, the smaller is likely to be the range of the S. Averaging the figures obtained in I B 1 b of the outline for the two, three, four and five-voice fugues, respectively, will substantiate this observation. (See § 32 a).

4

5. All fugue S.'s in the WTC define tonality by beginning on the first or fifth note of the T. scale (the two notes most nearly related to the T.). The only exceptions: II 13 (leading tone to T. note); II 21 (appoggiatura to T. note).

6. It is interesting to observe how clearly the Non-mod. S.'s define the T. by stressing the important chords of the cadence (see §§ 10-12, 3 in each case). Another way of stressing these important functions (S.D., D. and T.) is to call attention to the leading tone of these chords (I 12 has all three; I 14 has leading tone of S.D. and D.). In minor S.'s the raised seventh degree is often stressed in close proximity to the unraised sixth (I 6, I 16, I 20); or some other interval which does not occur in any other scale may be stressed, such as the diminished fourth in I 4. The T. is usually carefully defined in Mod. S.'s also, before they modulate away to the D. key (see I 7, 18, 24).

7. The last note of the S. is sometimes a matter for dispute. The safest general rule is to choose that note which comes with the arrival of the T. chord in the final cadence. In the case of Mod. S.'s this note will coincide with the arrival of the T. chord in the D. key (I 7, the first B flat in the second measure is the final note). Notice that when the last note of the S. comes on the third beat in 4/4 time, the last note of the A. usually comes on the first beat, giving a sense of finality to the S.—A. taken as a pair (I 1, 8, 16). This is not true in the Mod. S. I 7, where the second half of the last measure makes a link leading back to the T. key (§ 14). The more usual place for the S. to end is on the first beat, as will be observed in I 2, 3, 4, 5, 6. How Bach maintains continuity at these downbeats will be discussed in § 16.

8. It is often difficult to separate the rhythmic characteristics from the melodic, since the two are often so interrelated. To understand the structure of a Bach S. it is essential that the student learn how to divide it into rhythmic (or melodic) phrases or cells which are to any extent independent of one another. Then it is important to observe what means are used to make these phrases or cells adhere to one another, so that the S. gives the impression of perfect continuity. Intelligent phrasing is of the utmost importance in performance. Bach is often unintelligently phrased, both by performers and editors. The student who wishes to write a good S. must develop the ability to punctuate and thus clarify his ideas without destroying the continuity. There are a number of ways by which continuity may be achieved, especially important where the main points of punctuation occur; at the ends of preliminary phrases. Feminine endings are illustrated at the end of the first phrase of I 7, 16, 20 (see also §§ 10 and 12, 5 b in each case); sometimes the first phrase ends with more rhythmic solidity, but, on a note not contained in the T. chord, as in I 4, 5, 9, 12; sometimes the motion is even quicker after this critical point, as in I 6; or the general motion continues without interruption, as in I 10, 11, 12, 17. There are often rhythmic characteristics as well as melodic, which should be easily recognizable on rehearing.   Such characteristics should occur at various points along the line, making a number of features which may attract attention to the S.

9. The study of melody may limit itself more to the actual kinds of melodic motion, scalewise or by skips, that give the S. its character. The climactic note of each phrase should be carefully sought, and a decision made as to which of these notes should be considered the climax of the whole S. Rhythmic factors may contribute to this decision, as well as melodic and harmonic. The last note of the S. can scarcely be the climax, though the last note of the first phrase sometimes is, giving for that reason the impression that this phrase is incomplete and that the S. must continue (I 9, 13). The first note of the S. or of the phrase is seldom the climax, as nothing points to it (but see I 19).

10. Analysis of S. I 1, numbered according to the Outline, I B:

1. *a.* No. of voices: 4.
   b. Range: 9 semitones (major 6th).
2. Note of T. scale at start: 1.
3. Harmony shown above. Other harmonizations may suggest themselves, but, as in most S.'s, the chief chords of the cadence are suggested: ii or IV—V—I.
4. *a.* Ends on 3rd degree of T. on 3rd beat (see § 7).
   b. Non-mod. S.
5. *a.* Phrasing shown above.
   b. Continuity factors: first phrase ends on 4th beat, not decisively; second phrase begins immediately, only an eighth note later; the first two notes of the 2nd phrase are aimed at by two divergent lines in the first phrase; no fragment of either phrase gives a feeling of completeness. This S. might be said to be punctuated by a comma.
   c. Characteristics: the three eighths leading to a dotted eighth; the thirty-second note turn-around; the three notes stressed by skips at the start of the 2nd phrase; the syncopation; the three sixteenths leading to the final note.
6. *a.* Climaxes marked above; the main climax is in the second phrase, approximately two-thirds of the way through the S. The first F is the longest note of the first phrase, also the highest but for the short G, and it is a note not contained in the T. chord, making it fresh. The D of the second phrase is on a strong beat; it is approached by the longest skip which, though downward, still throws emphasis; a strong change of harmony is implied at this point; the first phrase aims at the D, and the arrested motion on the final E of this phrase tends to create tension and increase the emphasis on the D when it finally comes; Bach substantiates this by making a suspension at this point, which resolves as the G arrives.
   b. Rhythmic characteristics have already been mentioned, as also the skips. It is important to note that in the second phrase the upbeat motion to the climax is only one-third as long as the upbeat motion to the climax of the first phrase.

11. Analysis of S. I 2.

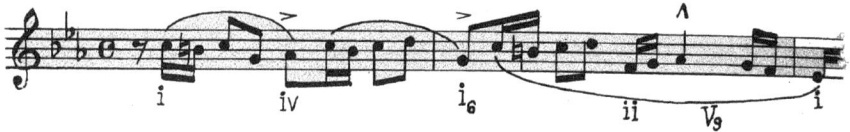

1.*a.* No of voices: 3.
  b. Range: 11 semitones (major 7th).
2. Note of T. scale at start: 1.
3. See above.
4.*a.* Ends on 3 of T. on downbeat.
  b. Non-mod. S.
5.*a.* See above
  b. The first two phrases seem to lack completeness, since it is not likely that the note of greatest stress, on which each phrase ends, will be conclusive. The last phrase is the only one which is rounded off. One of the most important continuity factors arises from the fact that the line is suddenly carried off by sixteenth note motion just at the point where the rhythmic pattern appears to be completed for the third time. The concluding part of the third phrase is thereby knit so closely to the first part that it has to be taken as one span. We have two short phrases followed by a phrase twice as long. This type of phrase management may be observed frequently in the works of Haydn, Mozart, Beethoven and others. The human mind welcomes a change in the length of the span of attention. It is effective to go from a shorter to a longer span.
  c. The rhythmic formula of two sixteenths, and three eighths; the surprising syncopation near the end which saves the S. from sounding mechanical.
6.*a.* The last A flat, because of its peculiar rhythmic emphasis. The half beats before beats 2 and 4 have been made very light up to this point, being given a feeling of upbeat motion; the turn-about of the trend of melody, which is chiefly downward from the first A flat to the final E flat, makes the syncopated A flat very conspicuous; A flat has been avoided for quite a time, in spite of its being stressed at the end of the first phrase.
  b. The two D's are extraordinary strokes of genius. Substituting F for the first, and E flat for the second, makes a very uninteresting S. The second time the D is particularly expressive, being out of the harmony.

12. Analysis of S. I 3:

1.*a.* No. of voices: 3.

  b. Range: 16 semitones (major 10th).

2. Note of T. scale at start: 5.

3. See above.

4.*a.* Ends on 1 of T. on downbeat.

  b. Non-mod. S.

5.*a.* See above. The three descending 7ths are much like a scale passage, not tending to throw particular stress on one note above another. The three taken together give the impression of a single phrase of the S. and seem to have a purely conclusive function.

  b. The first phrase ends on a weak beat (feminine ending). The last phrase is very masculine in its determined motion from upbeat to downbeat.

  c. See 5 *b.* Long upbeat motion in first phrase, followed by short upbeat motion in second. This S. reverses the idea of the S. in I 2: after a longer span the mind is relieved by a shorter span consisting of three very short fragments.

6.*a.* Judging by Bach's treatment of this S. it is apparent that he felt the note G sharp at the beginning of the second measure to be of great importance. It is subsequently set off as a dissonant note almost every time it appears. It comes on a downbeat, at the moment of an important implied change of harmony. Though it is a note of the T. chord (less often the note of greatest stress, as we shall find after completing this study), it is set off in new surroundings.

  b. The turn at the beginning, the leap up, the decorated resolution of the dissonance, and the descending sevenths are all recognizable characteristics.

7. If the break between phrases should be taken after the downbeat of the second measure, a repetition of the same pattern would occur: four ascending skips — much too monotonous an interpretation to please Bach.

13. There are two kinds of A.'s to Non-mod. S.'s. If each note of the A. is a perfect 5th above (or a perfect 4th below) the corresponding note of the S. we have a *real A.* (Examples: I 1, 4, 5, 6, 9). If the fifth note of the scale is emphasized at or near the start of the S. (before a change of harmony from the T. chord is implied) this note is usually answered by the T. note, making a *tonal A.* (Examples: I 2, 8, 11, 12). The tonal answer makes it possible for the beginning of the A. to fit the T. chord, when a real A. would not permit this. Thus a contrast in feeling between the S. and A. is created, the S. beginning and ending in the T. key, the A. starting in the T. key and modulating to the D. key. Thus a feeling of *tonal stability* in the S. is followed by a feeling of *tonal march* in the A., a valuable asset in providing a contrast between the two.

14. A Mod. S. may also have a real (I 18) or tonal (I 7, 24) start, the tonal start being necessary when the fifth note of the T. scale is emphasized as explained in § 13. The S. makes a modulation to the D. key, hence it is sometimes necessary to add a link to permit the beginning of the A. on the T. (I 7). The A., to avoid further modulation to the D. of the D. key, drops one tone at some point where it will least damage the theme (I 7, 18, 24). After the drop, each note of the A. is a perfect 4th above (or perfect 5th below) the S. Thus in the case of a Mod. S. we have *tonal march* followed by *tonal stability;* it is almost like reversing the more normal order when the S. is Non-mod.

15. The first note of the A. may coincide in time with the arrival of the last note of the S., but seldom does the A. begin more than a measure later. If the A. starts before the S. is finished, it is called a stretto fugue, the only example in the WTC being II 3.

16. The last note of the S. is usually at a point where conclusive harmony may be felt. From the standpoint of continuity of motion, it is a danger point. It is interesting to see how smoothly Bach continues the line from the S. after its final note (see I 1, 2, 3, 4, 5).

17. Many of Bach's fugues have a C.S. (a few more than one). These are usually written in invertible counterpoint so that they may be put above or below subsequent entrances of the S. or A. The C.S. usually has definite, recognizable characteristics of rhythm and melody, but it is carefully fashioned so as to set off to advantage the salient features of the S. (see I 2, 3, 7, 11, 13, 15; two C.S.'s I 21).

18. Some of Bach's fugues have no C.S. (Examples: I 1, 5, 17). In the case of a two-voice fugue a C.S. may make for monotony. Many of the three-voice fugues have C.S.'s, fewer of the four-voice fugues in the WTC. Possibly the confusion of so many voices makes a C.S. less obvious, hence less useful. (In I 18 the C.S. is used five times when no more than three voices are active, three times with all four present.)

19. Bach's fugues are quite varied in their construction. The three fugues which most nearly follow the pattern of the so-called *scholastic fugue* are I 16, 13, and 7, in that order. The parts of the fugue which one is likely to find in analysing the fugues of the WTC are listed in the outline (under IV).

20. The Main Exp., which is always present, continues until the last voice has finished his entrance of the S. or A.

21. In the Main Exp. (and only there) a general rule holds that if one numbers the voices from the top down, a S. in an odd voice is followed by an A. in an even voice, and *vice versa*. Moreover, in the case of the first pair: S.—A.. these are in adjacent voices (for the sake of unity). The only exceptions to the above in the three-part fugues are in fugues II 3 and 4, where the order is 312. In 13 fugues the voices enter 123; in 11, 213; in 2 others, 321. The order of entrance in the three-part fugues is invariably S.A.S. In the four-part fugues there is no exception to the first rule given above, the arrangements, in diminishing order of frequency, being: 3214, 2143, 4321, 2134, 3241, 3412. Exceptional orders of entrance occur only in I 1 (S.A.A.S.); and in I 12, 14 and II 23 (S.A.S.S.). In the two five-part fugues, the order is 54321 and 12345 (S.A.S.A.S.).

22. There is often a link between the first A. and the second S., permitting a modulation back to the original key when the S. is Non-mod.

23. When the S. or A. returns after the Main. Exp. is completed on its original notes, it is proper to call this a C. Exp. Quite frequently a C. Exp. follows the Main Exp. immediately, especially in the case of three part fugues (in which case the Ep. mentioned in IV B is often omitted). C. Exp.'s often occur at later points in the fugue (see I 2, 3, 7).

24. The various Ep.'s which come between the Exp.'s may use new material, or materials taken from the S. or C.S. They often increase in

importance and interest, leading to a final, Main Ep. in which more
and more startling contrapuntal devices may be introduced, such as all
sorts of combinations of S., A. and C.S. with inversions, retrograde
motion, augmentation and diminution. If this Main Ep. is to be followed by stretti, it is wise to avoid much use of the head of the S.,
since the stretti call much attention to these first notes of the S.
The first Ep.'s usually contrast with the Exp.'s in giving a greater
feeling of tonal march. However, it is very rare that we find Bach
leaving the six most nearly related keys: T., D., S.D., and their
Rel.'s, even during the Ep.'s. The Ep.'s should act as offsets to the
Exp.'s, making the S. or A. seem fresh when it comes in the next Exp.
25. There are naturally fewer entrances of S. or A. in related keys
than in the T. and its D. After the Main Exp. no usual order of entrance is followed. The Exp. in the Rel. may begin with an A. or a S.
In I 1 *12* and I 7 *17*, for example, an A. comes first, followed only in
the latter case by a S. The Exp. in the S.D. comes almost invariably
after the Exp. in the Rel., since the underlining of the S.D. area
gives rise to a feeling of finality. Often the Exp. in the S.D. is
omitted in favor of an Exp. in the Rel. of the S.D. (I *17 17*). I 21
has both: *26* and *35* in Rel. of S.D.: *37* in S.D. It is rare to find an
A. in the Exp. in the S.D., since the A. is likely to be also a S. in
the original key, making a C. Exp. However, there is obviously an A.
in the S.D. in I 5 *12* and *13*; and in I 21 *41* where the tonal A. proves
his intention. When the S. or A. does not fit the corresponding notes
of another scale, it should not be considered part of an Exp., but
rather a free imitation (Examples: I 1 *14* tenor voice; I 1 *19-20* tenor
and alto). For his own reasons (worth studying) Bach sometimes puts a
S. in the form of the A. (I 3 *14* in the Exp. in Rel.) or the A. in
the form of the S. (I 3 *19* also in Rel.). Other examples: I 8 *19-26;*
I 21 *35* (Exp. in Rel. of S.D.). Such examples should be considered as
parts of Exp.'s, since they follow the corresponding notes of the
scale except for the difference at the beginning.
26. There is not likely to be more than one Ped. in a fugue, either
on the D. (I 3 *37-40;* I 15 *62-64:* II 15 *56-66*); or on the T. (I 1 *24*
combined with Exp. in S.D. in stretto; I 2 *29½*). It is safer to begin
Ped.'s on the first beat of the measure, otherwise they may not seem
to arrive with conviction. In I 2 the bar lines do not have their
present-day significance.
27. Stretti may appear much earlier in the fugue than appears in the
Outline (I 8 *20*, I 15, *51* before the Exp. in S.D.). It is, however, a
climactic device to have the S. tumble closer on top of itself, and it
is well placed toward the end of the fugue. Other samples of stretti
may be found in I 8 *52-54*, *68-82* with Aug. and Inv.; I 11 *26-30,*
37-44; I 16 *28,29;* II 7 *30-42, 59-64.* Other examples of Inv.'s: I 8
30-50, 54-55; I 5 Ep. of *9, 10* Inv. *17*-on; II 6 *17, 18.*
28. Bach does not always put a final statement near the end, but he
always manages to make a strong harmonic cadence, which includes the

stressing of the three functions of the tonality: S.D., D. and T. This is sometimes done over a T. Ped. (I 2; I 15), more often by a strong bass line to the final chord.

29. The purpose of making a diagram is to call attention to the larger aspects of the form of a piece of music, as well as to some of the more detailed, in a way which is clearer to the eye than if one looks at the music itself. It is time-saving to obtain large sheets of graph paper with quarter-inch squares, which may be cut in strips and pasted on a card sufficiently long to permit the entire fugue to go on one line. Cut out one strip with as many horizontal lines as there are voices, and at least one vertical line for each bar. Sometimes 2 or 3 squares to the bar may be helpful. Paste this strip on the card, and one half inch below it paste a second strip of the same length having six horizontal lines.

Method of making diagram

a. Put bar numbers between the pasted strips.

b. Put a symbol (such as xxx) at each point where you find a complete S. or A. stated on its original notes or transposed to the corresponding notes of some other key. Trace voice lines to make sure these entrances are put on the proper line, since sometimes voices cross. Only after you have completed the rest of your diagram should you mark S. and A. (see f).

c. If there is a C.S., insert it wherever it occurs, using some such symbol as ooo.

d. On the lower strip make a graph of the keys through which the fugue goes. A sudden modulation may be shown by a vertical line, up or down, as in bar 22 of the example on next page. When there is common territory between keys, slant the line, as in measure 5, p. 11. Note how it is possible to interpret the same chord in two ways, during the period of common territory (in measure 5). or to interpret sudden changes of key which immediately return to the original key as the underlining of chords in that key (measures 14 and 20). Important cadences may be noted under the proper key line. It is useful to show on the graph cases where definite characteristics of a new key are shown, even though the time spent in that key be brief. This makes it more evident how Bach succeeds in maintaining a balance about the main key (see g). In the case of major fugues, arrange the keys in the same order as shown below, the Rel. minor always below its major, the D. keys above, the S.D. keys below. The below arrangement would be the right one for E flat major as well as for c minor.

e. Label the various parts of the fugue above the upper strip, calling attention to thematic elements upon which episodes are built.

f. Mark S.'s and A.'s. Call attention to any case where a S. appears in the form of the A. or vice versa (§ 25, end). Fill in with a straight line any points where the lines of the voices are free: not singing a strict version of S. or A. or a strict or even free version of the C.S. (The C.S. sometimes jumps from one voice to another, as in bars 26-28 of the example on page 11). Leave space where a voice rests (see measure 7).

g. At the end of each voice line put in the total number of entrances in each voice (to see how fair Bach has been to each of the voices). At the end of each key line put the total number of measures in each key. In many of the fugues the balance between the time spent in the D. keys and time spent in the S.D. keys is surprisingly even. Though the fugue on the next page goes for a short time into F major, this is quite exceptional. Bach usually stays within the 6 nearly related keys.

§30

Diagram: Bach Well-tempered Clavichord
Volume I, No.2 in c minor

Legend { S. or A. = xxxxx
C.S. = ooooo
Freer lines —

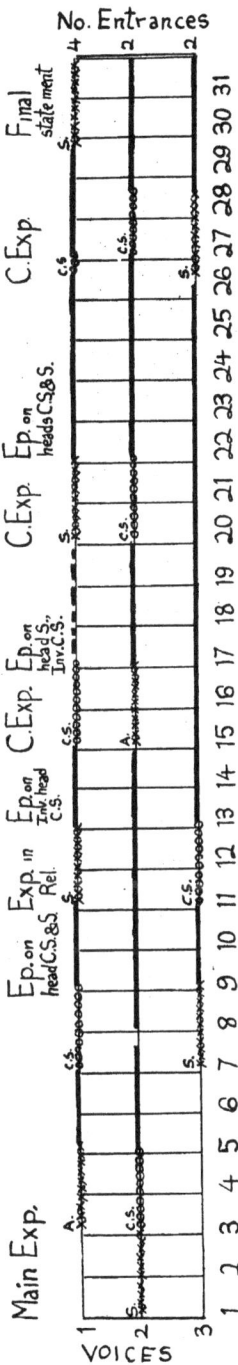

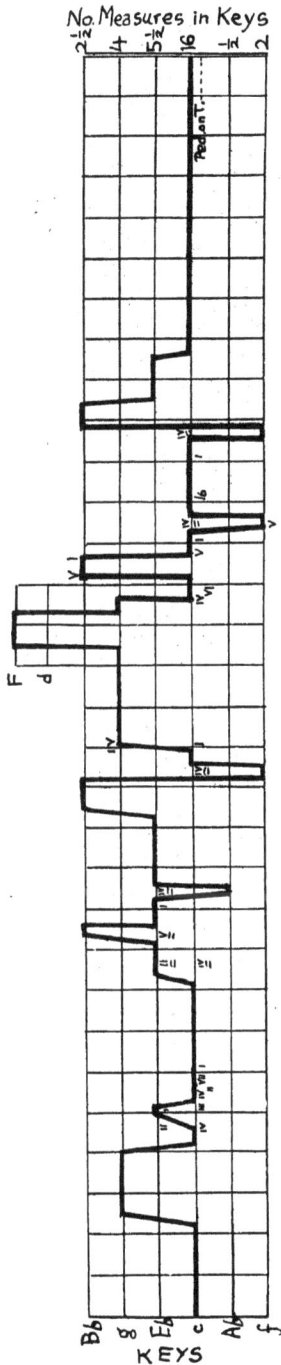

No. Entrances

Main Exp.   Ep.on head C.S.&S.   Exp. in Rel.   Ep.on Inv.head C.S.   C.Exp.   Ep.on head S., Inv.C.S.   C.Exp.   Ep.on heads C.S.&S.   C.Exp.   Final statement

VOICES
1
2
3

1 2 3 4 5 6 7 8 9 10 11 12 13 14 15 16 17 18 19 20 21 22 23 24 25 26 27 28 29 30 31

No. Measures in Keys

$-2\frac{1}{2}$ 4 $5\frac{1}{2}$ 16 $-1\frac{1}{2}$ 2

Pedant.

KEYS
Bb
g
Eb
c
Ab
f

Other fugues in WTC practical to diagram: I 1, 3, 5, 7, 8, 11, 13, 15, 16, 17, 18, 21; II 5, 6, 7, 15, 19, 20.

31. A student should write a good number of S.'s before attempting to write a fugue, and these should be criticised and revised until they are in as sturdy a shape as possible. Each should be as varied in character as possible. The following sums up some points which will have been gleaned in the study of Bach's own S.'s, and may be of some use to the student in his endeavours to write good S.'s in this style.

32. *a. Range* proportionate to number of voices (§ 4). The average range for 3-part fugues in the WTC is 11.1 semitones (a major 7th, plus); for 4-part fugues, 9.8 semitones (a minor 7th, minus); for the two 5-part fugues, 8.5 semitones (between a major and minor 6th). The only 2-part fugue has a range of 14 semitones (a major 9th). A 9th or a 10th is a safe limit for 3-part fugues; an 8ve for 4-part.

b. Scalewise motion is a valuable asset, making a line easy to follow. Skips should be purposeful, for emphasis or expressive gain, or as recognizable elements in design. A note approached or left by a skip must usually be treated as a note of the chord; a note in scalewise motion can fit a variety of circumstances, allowing freer treatment. Every note should appear to have a reason for existence in the general contour.

c. Bizarre skips, anticipations are difficult contrapuntally, especially in the style of Bach—yet an anticipation may make a recognizable characteristic of a motive (the only example in the WTC in a S. is II 21).

d. Several *changes in direction* make for greater ease in handling other voices. *Returning in the opposite direction after one or more skips* follows a natural melodic law. *Repetition of notes* should be done for the most part for expressive emphasis.

e. A *climactic note* is advisable in each phrase—often best if not a note of the T. chord. According to the author's analysis of all the fugue S.'s of the WTC, the main climax of the S. is a note of the T. chord in only 9 cases. 14 times it occurs on the 6th note of the scale, 10 times on the 4th degree, 7 times on the 2nd, 5 times on the 7th, etc. The *main climax* should not be too far from the end.

33. Definition of key (see § 6). The S. should suggest II or IV as well as V. Don't *stall* on one chord, but keep harmonies moving sufficiently to allow interesting possibilities for other voices. *Varied possibilities of harmonization* are valuable. *Strong root progressions* offer more chances for variety. Strong progressions: root 5th down or 4th up; root 3rd down; root a 2nd up. In each case a new root appears. Weaker progressions: root 5th up, 3rd up, a 2nd down. A subordinate member of the old chord becomes the ruler of the new one. Study the root progressions in I 5 (continue for 10 or 12 measures to understand the above point). It is good to mix in some weak progressions, or to combine a weak with a strong, to make a total of strength (such as: root a 3rd up—5th down: the total, root 3rd down). One may tire of all strong progressions, but they are very useful where feeling of strong progress ahead is desirable. When modulations are being made, strong progressions make them sound more inevitable.

34. The *rhythmic formulas* are often the *most easily recognized features* of the S. Even with changes in melodic steps, the idea may still sound congruous if the rhythmic pattern is characteristic. It is helpful to arrange a *rhythmic scheme which throws stresses at different points in different measures*. Study I 2, 6, 8, 14, 18 and others from this standpoint. It is *dangerous to repeat a rhythmic formula more than once*. Rhythmic means should be useful in stressing climaxes. To obtain *perfect continuity* plus *proper punctuation* to set off phrases and cells with clarity is a rhythmic problem, solved by Bach in numerous ingenious ways (review your findings under I B 5 *c*, and see § 5). See § 7 concerning the proper points at which to end S.

35. While working on S.'s it is always well to investigate the possibilities of the A. It is possible to write a plausible sounding S. to which the A. is quite uninteresting or awkward. On the other hand, see how much added expressiveness some A.'s have, often due to the Ton. A. (See I 8, 16, and especially 22, where the climax of the A. appears to be on another note: the fourth note instead of the third).

36. See § 18. Test C.S. for invertibility as you write it. Sometimes a C.S. may invert itself at some interval other than the 8ve, such as the 12th, which makes the C.S. equally useful. It is a good idea to practice inversions at more than one interval.

37. The Ep.'s should appear to be more restless tonally. Figure out where they should lead, and make a reasonable harmonic scheme which may be suggested by the lines. Material for early Ep.'s may come from the end of the S., or from the C.S., or may be new, contrasting with the chief rhythmic formulas of the S. Later Ep.'s may develop from other features of the S. (See § 24. The *Table of Modulations*, § 39, may be helpful in planning modulations. This table includes any one of the 18 conceivable modulations between the six nearly related keys, to which Bach customarily limits the fugues of the WTC).

38. Keep track of how much emphasis is being placed on each of the six keys, making a fairly even balance between the D. and S.D. keys. Incidental modulations during later expositions of S. and A. may add interest (to II or IV or D. or relative keys). Beginning or ending the S. or A. in an unexpected key may be rewarding, but all modulations should be smooth and convincing. Every line of every voice must appear purposeful; it must continuously aim for and stress notes which are fresh. One is by no means to be limited to the middle two octaves of the instrument. Modulations are important as a means of changing the function of the various notes, giving a new meaning to a note just previously heard in another key.

39. Modulations to nearly related keys.

A modulation can be divided roughly into three parts:

1. *Point of departure.*
2. *Change of scale.*
3. *Establishment of new key.*

Part 1 includes what may be considered as being in either the old or the new key: common territory between the two keys. The chords may tend toward those more famous in the second key, even before part 2 is reached. 2 begins at the point where a definite characteristic of a new key is introduced. In part 1 it is best to avoid the note (or notes) of the old scale to be altered, especially if a convincing rather than a temporary change of key is desired. Part 3 usually consists of a complete or partial cadence to strengthen the position of the new key.

Modulations 1-10, below, require the change of only one accidental in the signature. In these, part 2 may be only the point where the new accidental is introduced. Modulations 11-18 (in which the signature is changed by two accidentals) may also be made in a similar manner, though there is less common territory to be found. These latter modulations may also be made by combining two simpler modulations, the middle key being transient in feeling. In such cases the entire time spent in the second key may be considered as in part 2 of the modulation.

In approaching (and staying in) minor keys, great care must be taken to observe the tendencies of the 6th and 7th scale steps, whether raised or unraised. These four 'turning-notes' must be treated with care, otherwise a modulation away from the minor key in question will almost invariably occur (a fact which may very well be taken advantage of when one wishes to leave the key). *It does not matter how you approach the turning-notes. It matters how you leave them.* The raised 7th must go up to the 1st degree, the raised 6th to the raised 7th. They were only raised to go up, in imitation of the major scale, and they must not be doubled. The unraised 6th must descend to the 5th degree, the unraised 7th to the unraised 6th. It is dangerous to double the unraised turning-notes, especially in contrapuntal music. In 4-part writing it might be expedient to double an unraised turning-note, in which case it is safest to have the more conspicuous voice descend according to its tendency.

In the table below, triads (Roman numerals) and scale degrees (figures) of the *goal key* which make common territory with the first key are set down. In a minor key a triad containing a turning-note appears in *italics*. A scale degree which is a turning-note is likewise in *italics*. An *r* before either means it is a raised turning-note, otherwise it is unraised. Major triads are in capitals, minor in lower case. 'd' stands for diminished.

TABLE

No.	Mod. such as	Triads 2nd key common to 1st	Scale degrees ditto
1	C-G	I, ii, IV, vi	1,2,3,4,5,6
2	C-F	*I*, iii, V, vi	1,2,3, 5,6,7
3	C-a	i, d*ii*, III, *iv*, *v*, VI, VII	1,2,3,4,5,6,7
4	C-e	i, III, *iv*, VI	1, 3,4,5,6,7
5	C-d	i, *rii*, III, *rIV*, V, dr*vi*, VII	1,2,3,4,5,*r*6,7
6	a-C	all	all
7	a-e	same as No. 3	1,2,3,4,5,6,7
8	a-d	same as No. 5	1,2,3,4,5,*r*6,7
9	a-G	all	all
10	a-F	I, iii, V, vi	1,2,3, 5,6,7

ERRATA

Pages 14 and 15, the following lines should be substituted in the TABLE of modulations:

No.	Mod. such as	Triads 2nd key common to 1st	Scale degrees ditto
5	C-d	i, *rii, III, rIV, v, drvi, VII*	1,2,3,4,5,r6,7
13	C-b	*iv, VI*	1, 3,4, 6,7
14	C-g	*rii, rIV, v, VII*	1,2, 4,5,r6,7
18	a-g	*rii, v, rIV, rV, VII, drvii*	1,2, 4,5, 7,r7

Page 16, §41, line 1: 'changes' for 'change'.

No	Mod. such as	Triads 2nd key common to 1st	Scale degrees ditto
11	C-D	ii, IV	1,2, 4,5,6
12	C-Bflat	iii, V	2,3, 5,6,7
13	C-b	*iv, vi*	1, 3,4, 6,7
14	C-g	*rii, v, VII*	1,2, 4,5,r6,7
15	a-D	I, ii, IV, vi	1,2,3,4,5,6
16	a-Bflat	iii, V	2,3, 5,6
17	a-b	i, *III, iv, rIV, VI,* d*rvi*	1, 3,4, 6,r6
18	a-g	*rii, v, rV, VII,* d*rvii*	1,2, 4,5, 7,r7

KEY TO TABLE OF MODULATIONS

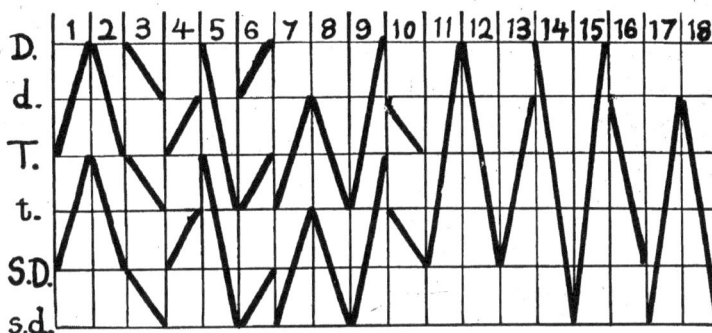

40. Following is a list of common 'mistakes' made by students in writing fugues. They may be taken as a list of 'don'ts' by the student, or they may be used by the teacher in correcting fugues, to save himself the time of a more lengthy explanation of the fault. References are made to sections where suggestions or hints may be appropriate. The mistakes are listed more or less in the order of frequency of occurrence, according to the experience of the author in teaching this style of counterpoint.

Common mistakes

1. 4th or 6-4 not rightly treated § 41
2. a. Unfortunate repetitions in line § 43
   b. Line lacks direction § 38
3. Dissonance uncharacteristically treated § 41
4. Bad melodic skip(s) § 43
5. Modulation unconvincing § 39
6. Rhythm mechanical §§ 34, 42
7. Bad direct unison, 8ve or 5th § 42
8. Syncopation held too long § 45
9. Bad anticipation § 32c
10. Cadence too weak § 28
11. Lack of continuity §§ 8, 34
12. Consecutive 8ves § 42
13. Too long a wait after stopping at a weak rhythmic point § 45
14. Thin § 41
15. Two voices skip in same direction § 42
16. Consecutive 5ths § 42
17. Lack of rhythmic independence § 42
18. Illogical changes of accidental § 41
19. Voice lines too parallel § 42
20. Harmony suggested weak § 38
21. Bad crossing of voices § 43

General principles of contrapuntal writing

41. When the character of the harmonic relationships change abruptly, attention may be directed away from the lines of the voices, toward their harmonic relationships. The lines of a Bach fugue almost invariably suggest a plausible underlying harmonic scheme, and no student should be allowed to study fugue writing unless he has a good grounding in classic harmony. Mistakes above listed which tend to alter the harmonic background in a distracting way are Nos. 1, 3, 14, 18.

42. Though the contrapuntal style of Bach is not as 'pure' as that of a di Lasso or a Palestrina, due to the increasing importance given to the harmonic background, still the chief aims are carried out: that of making the lines of the voices keep their independence, both linearly and rhythmically. Mistakes 7, 12, 15, 16 and 19 show lack of independence of line: mistakes 17 and also 6 make for a loss of rhythmic independence.

43. Good counterpoint also implies that the lines shall have a good sense of direction. Mistakes such as 2 a and b tend to remove the feeling of counterpoint by removing the feeling of line. Mistake 4 makes the lines hard to follow, detrimental to counterpoint. Although Bach frequently crosses his voices, he does it with care that the crossing is evident and that the lines of the two voices are still clear to the listener. In writing for a keyboard instrument there are many crossings which may be obscure—though the same spot might seem all right if written, for example, for a group of different woodwind instruments.

44. Treatments of dissonances in Bach come under two chief categories: 1. Melodic treatments: where the dissonance is justified by the inevitability of the line as it moves from one point of agreement to another; or leads to a point of agreement, as in the case of an appoggiatura; and 2. Harmonic treatments: cases such as preparation and resolution of dissonances; the dissonance in one chord leading to a consonance in the succeeding chord; etc. Most of the characteristic treatments of dissonance are studied in courses in classic harmony, and mistakes such as 1, 3, 18 and 20 are usually the same mistakes that are made in harmony courses. The student must be careful to suggest by the motion of the voices plausible progressions of harmony.

45. *Rhythmic characteristics.* It is not often that Bach syncopates a note beyond the point where its weight will be carried by the beat or halfbeat which it crosses. A note begun on a halfbeat seldom extends beyond the next halfbeat; one which begins on the 3rd beat in 4/4 time rarely lasts beyond the next 3rd beat (see mistake 8). Likewise a voice which comes to rest on a note beginning on the 2nd beat in 4/4 time will begin a new phrase by the 4th beat of the same measure (see mistake 13). Only when a note begins on the downbeat may it last indefinitely. Likewise when a voice begins the last note of its phrase on a downbeat, it may wait indefinitely before beginning its next phrase. It is evident that in a three-part fugue no voice should be silent for too long a time, once the three voices have all entered.

Lightning Source UK Ltd.
Milton Keynes UK
UKHW02f2137170918
329069UK00030BA/1633/P